TEAM SPIRIT®

SMART BOOKS FOR YOUNG FANS

THE LOS ANGELES RAMS

BY

MARK STEWART

I0807059

Norwood House Press

Norwood House Press
2544 Clinton Street
Buffalo, NY 14224

All photos, including cover, courtesy of Getty Images, except: Rams/NFL (6, 16, 37), Ebony Media (7), Upper Case Editorial Services (8, 23, 24, 38, 43 top), Author's Collection (11, 22, 32, 34 left, 39, 42 both), Hunt Auctions (15), Cleveland Historical Society (20), U.S. Air Force (27), Prometheus Books (30), Republic Pictures (31), Bowman Gum Co. (34 right), Street & Smith Publications (35 top left), McFadden Publishing (41).

The memorabilia, artifacts, and media images that are pictured in this book are presented for educational and informational purposes and come from the collection of the author.

Art Director: Lisa Miley
Series Design: Ron Jaffe
Project Management: Upper Case Editorial Services LLC
Special thanks to Topps, Inc.

Cataloging-in-Publication Data

Names: Stewart, Mark, 1960 July 7-.
Title: The Los Angeles Rams / Mark Stewart.
Description: Third edition. | Buffalo, NY : Norwood House Press, 2026. | Series: Team spirit | Includes glossary and index.
Identifiers: ISBN 9781978576261 (pbk.) | ISBN 9781978576278 (library bound) | ISBN 9781978576285 (ebook)
Subjects: LCSH: Los Angeles Rams (Football team : 2016-)--Juvenile literature. | Los Angeles Rams (Football team : 2016-)--History--Juvenile literature. | St. Louis Rams (Football team)--Juvenile literature. | Los Angeles Rams (Football team : 1946-1994)--Juvenile literature.
Classification: LCC GV956.L6 S74 2026 | DDC 796.332'640977866--dc23

CPSIA compliance information: Batch #CSNHP26: For further information contact Norwood House Press at 1-800-237-9932.

Manufactured in the United States of America.

TABLE OF CONTENTS

CHAPTER	PAGE

ABOUT OUR GLOSSARY

In this book, there may be several words that you are reading for the first time. Some are sports words, some are new vocabulary words, and some are familiar words that are used in an unusual way. All of these words are defined on page 46. Throughout the book, sports words appear in **bold type**. Regular vocabulary words appear in ***bold italic type***.

MAKING THE RAMS

Football teams choose their names very carefully. The Los Angeles Rams are no ***exception***. They named themselves after an animal that puts its head down and tries to overpower its opponent. That is what a lot of football players like to do, too. The funny thing is that, for most of their history, the Rams have preferred to throw the ball over their opponents, or scamper around them, rather than meeting them head-on.

To make the Rams, you actually need to do all of those things—and do them well. The team is at its best when it is locked in a high-scoring contest. But it can also win a hard defensive battle. When players pull on the Rams jersey, they know that they must work together no matter what kind of game they are in.

This book tells the story of the Rams. Their fans include some of the world's most famous actors, musicians, and ***influencers***. That is part of the fun of going to see them play. However, once the game begins, the Rams are all business.

Matthew Stafford drops back to pass during a 2024 game. His ability to light up the scoreboard makes him a fan favorite.

BUILDING BLOCKS

Sports fans in three different cities have watched the Rams play championship football since the team joined the **National Football League (NFL)** in 1937. No other team in the league can say that. Their first stop was Cleveland, Ohio. The team's early stars included Johnny Drake, Chet Adams, Jim Benton, Ted Livingston, and Parker Hall, who was named the league's Most Valuable Player (MVP) in 1939.

The Rams struggled to win more than half their games until 1945, when a **rookie** named Bob Waterfield joined the club. He was a talented quarterback who also kicked field goals. The Rams found a perfect coach in Adam Walsh. He believed that strong-armed passers such as Waterfield were the future of football. The Rams went 9–1 in 1945 and won their first NFL championship.

A few months

later, fans were shocked to learn that the Rams were moving to Los Angeles, California. Dan Reeves, the team's owner, believed that the Rams would draw more fans on the west coast, where the population was growing rapidly. Other sports teams had thought of doing the same thing. The Rams were the first to actually take the chance. It turned out to be a great move.

The Rams had a star-studded team. Waterfield and Norm Van Brocklin shared time at quarterback. Waterfield usually played the first and third quarters, and Van Brocklin would come in for the second and fourth quarters. They had two excellent receivers in Tom Fears and Elroy "Crazy Legs" Hirsch. Three big running backs—Dan Towler, Tank Younger, and Dick Hoerner—made up the Rams' "Bull Elephant" backfield.

Towler and Younger were two of the NFL's top African American stars. At a time when there weren't many Black players in the league, the Rams were ***pioneers***. Other African American stars who took the field for Los Angeles included Kenny Washington, Woody Strode, Dick "Night Train" Lane, and Bob Boyd. The team reached the NFL championship game four times from 1949 to 1955. The Rams

LEFT: The 1945 Rams pose for a team photo.
ABOVE: Kenny Washington made headlines as a pioneering Black player (at a time when Black people were called "Negroes," which is a derogatory term, and not given the rights of white Americans) when he suited up for the Rams in 1946.

29

won the league title once, in 1951.

After a handful of losing seasons in the early 1960s, the Rams became competitive again. The key was their defensive line of Deacon Jones, Merlin Olsen, Rosey Grier, and Lamar Lundy—who together were known as the "Fearsome Foursome." They got help from linebackers Maxie Baughan and Jack Pardee and defensive backs Eddie Meador and Clancy Williams. Quarterback Roman Gabriel guided a strong offense that included receivers Jack Snow and Bernie Casey and running backs Les Josephson and Dick Bass.

Los Angeles won its **division** seven years in a row during the 1970s. The Rams reached the **Super Bowl** for the first time in 1980. Again, their defense led the way. Jack Youngblood, Fred Dryer, and Isiah Robertson were all hard-hitting stars. The offense relied on a balanced attack that featured receiver Harold Jackson and running back Lawrence McCutcheon.

The Rams continued their fine play during the 1980s. Their best player was Eric Dickerson. He was a tall, graceful running back with great speed and power. He was named the NFL Offensive Rookie of the Year in 1983 and rushed for more than 2,000 yards the following season.

In the early 1990s, the Rams struggled to play winning football. Unemployment in the region and an ***outdated*** stadium made it difficult to sell tickets. In 1995, the team moved nearly 2,000 miles

LEFT: Eric Dickerson

to St. Louis, Missouri. The city had been home to the Cardinals from 1960 to 1987 before they moved to Arizona. St. Louis fans adored their new high-scoring team, which they nicknamed the "Greatest Show on Turf."

Quarterback Kurt Warner had some of the NFL's best weapons, including running back Marshall Faulk and receivers Isaac Bruce and Torry Holt. No team in the NFL could match the Rams' firepower. In 1999, they took the championship of the **National Football Conference** (**NFC**) and then won Super Bowl XXXIV. It was the team's first title in almost 50 years. Two seasons later, they returned to the Super Bowl, but lost to the New England Patriots on a field goal in the final seconds.

The pride felt by St. Louis football fans began to fade in the years that followed. The Rams put many good players on the field, including quarterback Matt Bulger, running back Steven Jackson, and defensive lineman Robert Quinn. However, they were unable to find their old magic. After just one winning season from 2002 to 2015, the team left St. Louis and returned to Los Angeles.

This time, the fans came out in force to cheer for the Rams. More than 90,000 bought tickets to their first home game. After a

4–12 season in 2016, the team hired a young and ***innovative*** head coach, Sean McVay, who built a winning team around quarterback Jared Goff, running back Todd Gurley, receivers Robert Woods and Brandin Cooks, and a rock-solid defense led by defensive tackle Aaron Donald, who was named Defensive Player of the Year in 2018. That season, the Rams were NFC champions but lost the Super Bowl to the Patriots, 13–3.

Three years later, Los Angeles had a new quarterback, Matthew Stafford, and a strong supporting cast that included Cooper Kupp, who led the NFL with 145 receptions. The Rams made it back to the big game and beat the Cincinnati Bengals for their first championship since 1999.

LEFT: Kurt Warner and coach Dick Vermeil clap for team owner Georgia Frontiere during the Rams' Super Bowl celebration. **ABOVE**: Super Bowl stars Matthew Stafford and Cooper Kupp signed this photo.

8:47
Q2
14
3
Ball On 6
3rd & 3
Plays: 17 Pass Yds: 93 Rush Yds: 56 Total Yds: 149
Offense
RAMS
The
MS HOUSE

GAME DAY

For most of their time in Cleveland, the Rams played in a baseball stadium called League Park. After moving to California in 1946, they hosted their games in the Los Angeles Memorial Coliseum. In 1980, the team moved south to Anaheim Stadium, where it stayed through the 1994 season. In St. Louis, the Rams played in a domed stadium.

The Rams moved back into the Coliseum for four years after returning to California. The team's new stadium opened in 2020 to rave reviews. The Rams share it with the Chargers, who moved north from San Diego in 2017. The stadium has won many architectural awards and is one of the most fan-friendly in the world. In 2022, the Rams won the 2021 NFC championship game and Super Bowl LVI on their home field. It was the first time this had ever happened.

BY THE NUMBERS

- *The Rams' stadium has 70,240 seats for football.*
- *The stadium's roof is made of 302 panels; 46 can open and close to keep fans cool.*
- *In 2028, the stadium is scheduled to host events during the Summer Olympics, as well as the Paralympics.*

The Rams' stadium is the most modern in the NFL.

RAMS
NFL
8

TEAM COLORS

The Rams have used many different colors and uniforms over the years. In Cleveland, they wore red and black. In 1938, the team switched to yellow and blue. Ten years later, running back Fred Gehrke painted yellow rams' horns on his blue helmet. Before long, the whole team followed his lead. It was the first time an NFL team featured a ***logo*** on its helmet.

In 1964, the Rams replaced the yellow in their uniforms with white. In 1973, they went back to yellow. Several years after moving to St. Louis, the team changed the yellow to a metallic gold. A logo of a ram's head was also added to the uniform. After their return to Los Angeles, the Rams kept the same combination of colors and styles, and also added a bone-gray uniform color.

LEFT: Jared Verse wears the Rams' traditional yellow and blue uniform.
ABOVE: The team's famous helmet design dates back to 1948.

LAST TEAM STANDING

The Rams have been the "last team standing" in three different cities. Their first NFL championship came in Cleveland, in 1945. Rookie Bob Waterfield made a big splash that season. He topped all NFL quarterbacks with 14 touchdown passes, had six interceptions as a defensive back, and also served as the team's punter and kicker. His best receiver was Jim Benton. Fred Gehrke, Jim Gillette, and Don Greenwood were all talented running backs.

The Rams faced the Washington Redskins (now the Commanders) for the 1945 NFL championship game on a windy day in Cleveland. The Rams came alive in the second quarter when Waterfield threw a long touchdown pass to Benton. He tossed another in the third quarter, this time to Gillette. From there, the Rams tightened their defense and won, 15–14.

The team's next title came in 1951, after the

LEFT: Bob Waterfield was picked to be on the cover of the NFL Guide in 1946.
RIGHT: Dan Towler heads for the goal line against the Cleveland Browns in the 1951 title game.

Rams had moved to Los Angeles. Waterfield combined with Norm Van Brocklin to give the team a great passing attack. Together, they threw for 26 touchdowns in 12 games. Seventeen of those scoring tosses went to Elroy Hirsch. Dan Towler, Tank Younger, and Dick Hoerner handled the team's rushing duties.

In the 1951 NFL championship game, the Rams met the team that had replaced them in Cleveland, the Browns. They knew each other very well. One year earlier, the Browns had beaten the Rams for the league title on a last-second field goal. This time, Los Angeles made the big play. With the score tied late in the contest, Van Brocklin launched a long pass to Tom Fears. Fears cradled the ball and raced into the **end zone** for a 73-yard touchdown. The Rams held on for a 24–17 victory.

Nearly a half-century passed before the Rams flew their next championship banner. By then, the team had moved to St. Louis. In 1999, the Rams had the game's most exciting offense. Quarterback Kurt Warner led the league with 41 touchdown passes and was named NFL Most Valuable Player. Running back Marshall Faulk gained 1,381 yards on the ground and caught 87 passes for another 1,048 yards. Receivers Isaac Bruce and Torry Holt combined for 18 touchdowns. Kevin Carter, Todd Lyght, D'Marco Farr, and Grant Wistrom led the St. Louis defense.

The Rams faced the Tennessee Titans in Super Bowl XXXIV. They raced to a 16–0 lead and looked like they were in complete control. However, the Titans tied the score with two minutes left. Warner and Bruce came to the rescue. The pair hooked up on a 73-yard touchdown pass with time running out. The Titans stormed right back and nearly scored a last-second touchdown, but the St. Louis defense managed to stop them just short of the goal line. The Rams won 23–16 for the third championship in team history.

In 2021, the Rams won their fourth championship. They were back in California and rocking a brand-new stadium. Quarterback Matt Stafford and receiver Cooper Kupp powered the Los Angeles offense. Aaron Donald and Jalen Ramsey led the defense. The Rams defeated the Cardinals, Buccaneers, and Packers in the **playoffs** to win the NFC crown. Because the league had already scheduled the Super Bowl for their stadium, the Rams had the good luck to face Joe Burrow and the Cincinnati Bengals on their home field.

The two teams were evenly matched. The Rams held a slim lead at halftime, but the Bengals scored on their first two drives of the third quarter to make the score 20–13. Matt Gay booted a field goal for Los Angeles to close the gap to 20–16 heading into the fourth quarter.

Both teams played great defense as the final 15 minutes ticked away. The Rams had one last chance when they got the ball on their 21-yard line. Moments later, they faced a fourth-and-one that could have ended their season. Kupp fooled the Bengals when he took a handoff on an **end-around** and made the first down. Stafford hit Kupp with two more passes to move the Rams into scoring territory. Three penalties followed, giving the Rams the ball on the 1-yard line. Stafford threw a short pass to Kupp in the end zone for his eighth catch and second touchdown of the day with less than 1:30 on the clock. The Los Angeles defense prevented a comeback by Burrow and gave the team the 23–20 victory.

LEFT: Isaac Bruce spins away from a tackler on the way to his game-winning score in Super Bowl XXXIV. **ABOVE**: Cooper Kupp makes a leaping catch in the Super Bowl.

LEADING LIGHTS

Some players lead with their words. Others lead with their actions. The greatest Rams inspired their teammates and thrilled their fans by doing both. They are the team's brightest stars…

JIM BENTON — Receiver

• Born: 9/25/1916 • Died: 3/28/2001

• Played for Team: 1938 to 1940 & 1943 to 1947

At 6'3" and over 200 pounds, Jim Benton was one the largest receivers in the NFL. He was also one of the best. He was first-team **All-Pro** in the Rams' final season in Cleveland and their first in Los Angeles. Benton was big enough to play defensive end for the Rams, too.

PARKER HALL — Quarterback/Kicker

• Born: 12/10/1916 • Died: 2/8/2005

• Played for Team: 1939 to 1942

Parker Hall was the Rams' greatest star when they played in Cleveland. In 1939, he became the first pro to complete 100 passes in a season and was named league MVP as a rookie. Hall was also one of the NFL's best punters.

BOB WATERFIELD

Quarterback/Kicker

• BORN: 7/26/1920 • DIED: 3/25/1983 • PLAYED FOR TEAM: 1945 TO 1952

Bob Waterfield was the finest all-around player of his time. He was the NFL passing champion twice and the league's top field-goal kicker three times. Waterfield often punted the ball more than 60 yards, and he also intercepted 20 passes during his career.

NORM VAN BROCKLIN

Quarterback

• BORN: 3/15/1926 • DIED: 5/2/1983 • PLAYED FOR TEAM: 1949 TO 1957

Norm Van Brocklin had a strong arm and a great desire to win. He always demanded the best from his teammates. Van Brocklin was voted into the Hall of Fame in 1971.

ELROY HIRSCH

Receiver

• BORN: 6/17/1923 • DIED: 1/28/2004 • PLAYED FOR TEAM: 1949 TO 1957

Elroy Hirsch was nicknamed "Crazy Legs" for his wild running style. In 1951, he had one of the greatest seasons in history. Hirsch led the NFL with 66 catches, 1,495 yards, and 17 touchdowns.

DEACON JONES

Defensive Lineman

• BORN: 12/9/1938 • DIED: 6/3/2013 • PLAYED FOR TEAM: 1961 TO 1971

If an opponent limited Deacon Jones to one or two sacks in a game, it was considered a success. No one during the 1960s was better at getting to the quarterback. Not only was the quarterback sack a Jones specialty—he actually invented the name for it!

LEFT: Parker Hall

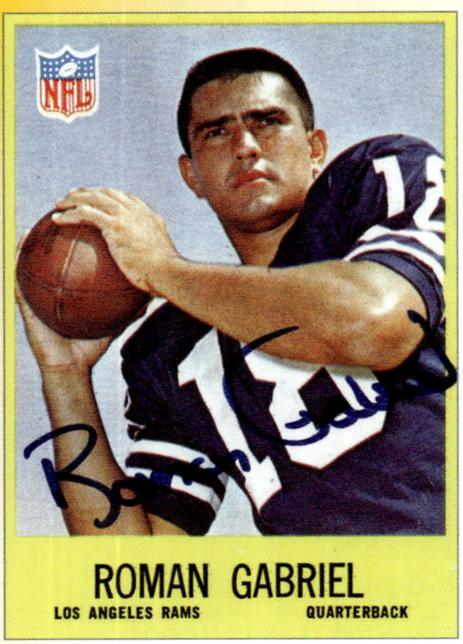

ROMAN GABRIEL — Quarterback

- Born: 8/5/1940 • Died: 4/20/2024
- Played for Team: 1962 to 1972

At 6'5", Roman Gabriel was the biggest quarterback of his era. In 1967, the Rams lost only one game behind him. In 1969, he opened the season with 11 wins in a row. Gabriel was named NFL MVP that season.

MERLIN OLSEN — Defensive Lineman

- Born: 9/15/1940 • Died: 3/11/2010
- Played for Team: 1962 to 1976

Merlin Olsen teamed up with Deacon Jones for 10 seasons on the defensive line. The two were an almost unstoppable pair. Olsen was named All-Pro 10 times and made the **Pro Bowl** in each of his first 14 seasons.

JACK YOUNGBLOOD — Defensive Lineman

- Born: 1/26/1950 • Played for Team: 1971 to 1984

Jack Youngblood carried on the Rams' tradition of great pass rushers. He had more than 150 sacks for Los Angeles and was a first-team All-Pro five times between 1974 and 1979. Youngblood served as defensive captain of the Rams for much of his career and set the team record for most games played in a row, with 201.

ABOVE: Roman Gabriel signed this 1960s trading card.
RIGHT: Eric Dickerson warms up before a game.

ERIC DICKERSON Running Back

• BORN: 9/2/1960

• PLAYED FOR TEAM: 1983 TO 1987

Eric Dickerson's size, speed, and toughness made him a nightmare for opposing defenses. He could power through defensive linemen and outrun defensive backs. In his first four seasons with the Rams, he gained nearly 7,000 yards and scored 57 touchdowns.

ISAAC BRUCE Receiver

• BORN: 11/10/1972

• PLAYED FOR TEAM: 1994 TO 2007

Isaac Bruce teamed up with Torry Holt to give the Rams a great receiving duo. He had an amazing ability to change his speed and direction. Bruce caught 119 passes in 1995 and scored the touchdown that won Super Bowl XXXIV for the Rams.

KURT WARNER Quarterback

• BORN: 6/22/1971 • PLAYED FOR TEAM: 1998 TO 2003

Kurt Warner developed a lightning-quick throwing style while playing in the **Arena Football League**. In the NFL, he was the league's top passer three years in a row. Warner was NFL MVP in 1999 and 2001.

MARSHALL FAULK — Running Back

• Born: 2/26/1973

• Played for Team: 1999 to 2005

Marshall Faulk was the most dangerous running back in the NFL when he played for the Rams. Every time Faulk took a handoff or caught a pass, he was a threat to go all the way. In 2000 and 2001, he scored a total of 47 touchdowns.

TORRY HOLT — Receiver

• Born: 6/5/1976

• Played for Team: 1999 to 2008

Torry Holt had breathtaking speed. He needed just the smallest opening in the defense to break free for a long gain. His best season came in 2003 when he had 117 receptions for 1,696 yards and 12 touchdowns. Holt finished behind Isaac Bruce as the team's all-time leading receiver.

STEVEN JACKSON — Running Back

• Born: 7/22/1983 • Played for Team: 2004 to 2012

Steven Jackson watched and learned from Marshall Faulk. However, while Faulk glided down the field, Jackson ran more like a bulldozer. He topped 1,000 yards every season from 2005 to 2012 and was voted to the Pro Bowl three times.

ABOVE: Marshall Fauk **LEFT**: Aaron Donald

AARON DONALD — Defensive Lineman

• Born: 5/23/1991

• Played for Team: 2014 to 2023

A lot of offensive linemen celebrated when Aaron Donald decided to retire after the 2023 season. Only a handful of defensive tackles in NFL history had his mix of power, speed, and quickness. Donald was named Defensive Player of the Year in 2017, 2018, and 2020. In 2019, he was named the number-one star in football in a vote of other NFL players.

COOPER KUPP — Receiver

• Born: 6/16/1993 • First Season with Team: 2017

Cooper Kupp was born to play pro football. His father was a quarterback for the Cardinals and Cowboys and his grandfather was a Pro Bowl offensive lineman. In 2021, Kupp had a season for the ages. He caught 145 passes and scored 16 touchdowns and was named MVP of Super Bowl LVI.

MATTHEW STAFFORD — Quarterback

• Born: 2/7/1988 • First Season with Team: 2021

When the Rams traded for Matthew Stafford, they believed he could do something he had been unable to accomplish in his years with the Lions: win a Super Bowl. Surrounded by offensive stars and supported by a great defense, Stafford guided Los Angeles to the big game in his first season—and won. Along the way he set new team records for completions and passing yards.

X'S & O'S

The man calling the shots for the Rams' first championship was Adam Walsh. He coached the team during its last year in Cleveland and then its first year in Los Angeles. Walsh was a pioneer. He believed that the quarterback was the most important player on offense. Using the **T-formation**, Walsh turned the Rams into champions. Quarterback Bob Waterfield and receiver Jim Benton both became stars under Walsh.

The Rams continued to be a high-scoring team in the 1950s. Their coaches during this ***decade***—Joe Stydahar, Hamp Pool, and Sid Gillman—loved the passing game, too. Stydahar and Pool both favored the long bomb. When they were in charge, the Rams could find the end zone from anywhere on the field. Under Gillman, the team experimented with short passes. He led the Rams to the NFL title game in his first season.

During the 1960s, 1970s, and 1980s, George Allen, Chuck Knox, Ray Malavasi, and John Robinson all coached the Rams to division titles. Los Angeles played in the NFC championship game

Sean McVay is rarely out of contact with his coaching staff.

seven times but only made it to the Super Bowl once, following the 1979 season.

In 1997, Dick Vermeil was hired to coach the Rams, who were now playing in St. Louis. He teamed with assistant coach Mike Martz to give the team a quick-strike offense that reminded many fans of the exciting Los Angeles teams of the 1950s. Vermeil led the Rams to victory in Super Bowl XXXIV in his third season. Martz took over as head coach and got the Rams back to the Super Bowl two years later.

In 2017, with the team back in Los Angeles, Sean McVay became the head coach. At the age of 30, he was the youngest coach in the NFL. Some fans worried that he lacked the experience to build a championship club. In his first year, the Rams went from the lowest-scoring team in the league to having the number-one offense—and made it back to the playoffs for the first time in 13 seasons. In 2018, McVay guided the team to the Super Bowl. In 2021, the Rams were NFL champions.

IN THE MOMENT

JANUARY 30, 2000

Heading into the 1999 season, fans of the Rams believed their team was the best in the NFL—as long as Trent Green was their quarterback. When he got hurt in the **preseason**, they panicked. Fortunately, backup passer Kurt Warner kept his cool. He surprised everyone by throwing for more than 4,000 yards and 41 touchdowns. Warner led the league's best offense into Super Bowl XXXIV against the Tennessee Titans.

The Tennessee defense was every bit as good as the St. Louis offense. In the first quarter, Warner moved the Rams into scoring position, but St. Louis had to settle for a field goal. The Rams added two more short kicks to make it 9–0 at halftime. Early in the third quarter, Tennessee lined up for a field goal of its own. Todd Lyght blocked the kick to give the ball back to St. Louis. Warner marched the team down the field and flipped a short pass to Torry Holt in the end zone. The Rams now led by a score of 16–0.

The Titans fought back and tied the score at 16–16. The Rams got the ball with just over two minutes left in the game. Warner

Mike Jones wraps up Kevin Dyson before he can stretch across the goal line.

dropped back to pass and saw Isaac Bruce open. With the Titans pressuring him, Warner lofted a wobbly pass to Bruce. He caught the ball in stride and sprinted the rest of the way for a touchdown. The Rams led, 23–16.

Again, the Titans fought back. They moved the ball to the St. Louis 10-yard line with enough time for one last play. Tennessee's Kevin Dyson caught a short pass and lunged for the goal line. Linebacker Mike Jones was waiting for him. He wrapped his arms around Dyson's legs and pulled him to the turf. Jones stopped Dyson just inches short of a touchdown.

The Rams were NFL champions for the first time since 1951. The difference between winning and losing came down to the final seconds and less than one yard. No Super Bowl had ever ended in such heart-stopping fashion.

WAIT . . . WHAT?

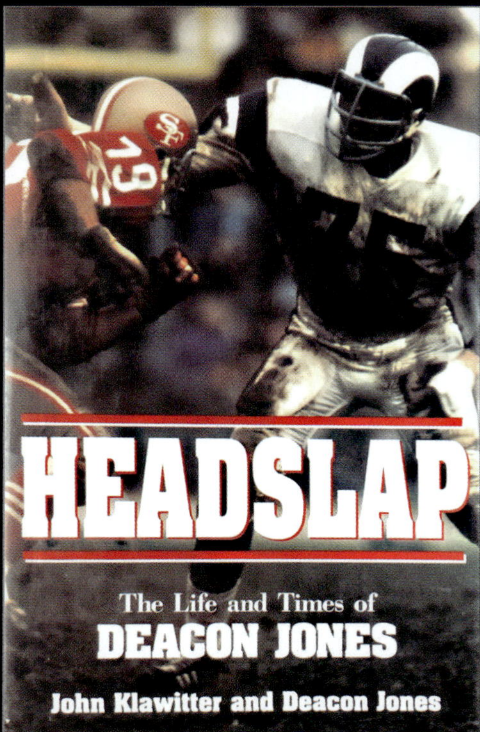

DID YOU KNOW?

A Rams superstar perfected a play that was later outlawed by the NFL. Defensive end Deacon Jones was big and fast. He also had lightning-quick hands. The instant the ball was snapped, he would whack the blocker in front of him on the helmet to make him blink—so he would miss Jones's pass-rushing move. He called it the "head slap." Jones did not claim he invented the move, but no one did it better. In 1977, the NFL announced that the head slap was no longer allowed. Even so, when Jones wrote the story of his life in 1996, he called the book *Head Slap*.

ABOVE: Deacon Jones named his book after the move that made him famous.
RIGHT: The movie poster for *Crazylegs* also featured four of Elroy Hirsch's Los Angeles teammates.

DID YOU KNOW?

A Ram once played himself in a movie about his life. In 1953, Elroy Hirsch was the star of *Crazylegs*. Hirsch had a big personality and it showed on screen. The film was fun and fast-paced, and was nominated for an *Academy Award*. It also promoted Hirsch's teammates, including several African American stars.

DID YOU KNOW?

Two other NFL teams tried to move to Los Angeles at the same time the Rams did. During the 2015 season, L.A. did not have a single pro football team. At the end of the year, the Rams, Oakland Raiders, and San Diego Chargers all asked the league if they could relocate to Los Angeles. The NFL agreed to consider the requests—as long as the teams were willing to pay $550 million to move. All three teams agreed, but there would only be room for two. The league chose the Rams and Chargers and told the Raiders to keep looking. They eventually moved to Las Vegas, Nevada.

UNBELIEVABLE!

There is no bigger challenge in the NFL than reaching the Super Bowl. The Rams found this out during the 1970s. Season after season, they went to the playoffs, but they always fell short of the Super Bowl.

In 1979, the Rams appeared to be going nowhere during the regular season. After 11 games, their record stood at 5–6. Things got worse when they were forced to use an untested third-year player named Vince Ferragamo at quarterback. He was playing only because Pat Haden had a badly broken finger.

Most fans gave up on the season. Ferragamo had a different idea. This was his big chance—and he took advantage of it. With Ferragamo leading the way, the Rams won their next four games. Los Angeles finished 9–7 and won the NFC West.

LEFT: Pat Haden's broken finger did not prevent him from signing this action photo. **RIGHT**: Vince Ferragamo prepares to throw a long pass.

Against the Dallas Cowboys in the playoffs, it looked like Ferragamo had run out of magic. In the first quarter, he was sacked in the end zone for a two-point ***safety***. Again, Ferragamo didn't quit. He threw two touchdown passes in the second quarter and another with two minutes left in the game. The Rams won 21–19.

One week later, Ferragamo and the Rams faced the Tampa Bay Buccaneers in the NFC championship game. The winner would advance to the Super Bowl. Tampa Bay had the league's toughest defense, but Ferragamo was up to the challenge. On three different drives, he moved the Rams close enough to kick a field goal. That was all they needed for a 9–0 victory. For the first time in their history, the Rams reached the Super Bowl—and they owed it all to a backup quarterback!

IT'S ABOUT TIME

In this timeline, each Super Bowl is listed under the year it was played. Remember that the Super Bowl is held early in the year and is actually part of the previous season. For example, Super Bowl LVI was played on February 13, 2022, but was the championship of the 2021 season.

1937
The team joins the NFL as the Cleveland Rams.

1945
The Rams win their first championship.

1946
The Rams move to Los Angeles.

1950
Tom Fears catches 18 passes in a game.

1969
Roman Gabriel is named NFL MVP.

1973
Harold Jackson leads the NFL with 13 touchdown catches.

This program is from the team's days in Cleveland.

Tom Fears

Jim Everett made the covers of many magazines in 1989.

Steven Jackson

1989
Jim Everett leads the NFL in TD passes.

1995
The Rams move to St. Louis, Missouri.

2000
The Rams win Super Bowl XXXIV.

2006
Steven Jackson leads the NFL with 2,334 total yards.

2018
Aaron Donald is named Defensive Player of the Year.

2022
The Rams win Super Bowl LVI

Rams' fans have been known to take team spirit to extremes.

THAT'S A FACT

FOLLOW THE BOUNCING BALL

In a 1994 game against the Saints, the New Orleans punter booted the ball into the back of the Rams' end zone and everyone on the field assumed it would keep going for a **touchback**. Everyone, that is, except Robert Bailey. The ball took a weird, backwards hop and no one bothered to down the ball. Bailey scooped it up and ran untouched 103 yards for the longest punt return in NFL history.

A CLOSE SECOND

Bob Waterfield was the most famous athlete on the Rams. In his own home, however, he was the second-most-famous person. Waterfield was married to superstar actress Jane Russell.

WHAT'S IN A NAME?

When Nigerian linebacker Nkama Ekubam joined the Rams in 2017, announcers were having trouble pronouncing his first name. The team suggested using his second name: Samson. Samson was a character in the Bible who defeated an entire army by himself.

LIGHT! CAMERAS! ACTION!

Because the Rams played in the television and movie capital of the country, many players appeared in episodes of popular television shows during the 1960s and 1970s. In the 1980s, two of their stars, Merlin Olsen and Fred Dryer, each starred in his own television series.

Dennis Harrah

BLOCK PARTY

Offensive linemen aren't usually considered team leaders in the NFL. Dennis Harrah was the exception. He served as the Rams' team captain for six seasons in the 1980s.

HARD TO CATCH

In 1949, Tom Fears set an NFL record with 77 pass receptions. The following year, Fears broke his own record with 84 receptions—including 18 in one game!

SIDELINED

In 1941, Jim Benton quit the Rams after three seasons to coach high school football in his hometown. He returned to the game after a year off and went on to be a first-team All-Pro in 1945 and 1946. On Thanksgiving Day in 1945, he set a new record with 303 receiving yards.

TALKING FOOTBALL

"Believe in yourself, even when others doubt you. Your belief is what will carry you through to victory."

COOPER KUPP, *on the importance of confidence*

"My vision is my best ***attribute.*** I can see everything."

MARSHALL FAULK, *on the key to his success as a running back*

"Big-time players make big-time plays in big-time spots. That's who I want to be."

AARON DONALD, *on his reputation as a game-changer*

ABOVE: Marshall Faulk scores against the Tampa Bay Buccaneers in the playoffs.
RIGHT: All four members of the Fearsome Foursome signed this photo.

"I am where I am because I believed and I never gave up."

KURT WARNER, *on his journey from grocery store worker to Hall of Famer*

"Put a football under Elroy's arm and he speeds up. Don't ask me how!"

JOE STYDAHAR, *on Elroy "Crazy Legs" Hirsch*

"I don't think there's a defensive line to this day—or will be in the near future—that'll have that much balance."

DEACON JONES, *on the "Fearsome Foursome"*

"The hardest part of the day for me was standing in that tunnel waiting for the game to get under way. I couldn't wait to get on the field."

MERLIN OLSEN, *on the excitement he felt before games*

ROAD TRIP

For fans of the Rams, all roads lead to Los Angeles. But each journey begins somewhere else. Match the pushpins on these maps to the Team Facts, and you will discover the ultimate Rams road trip!

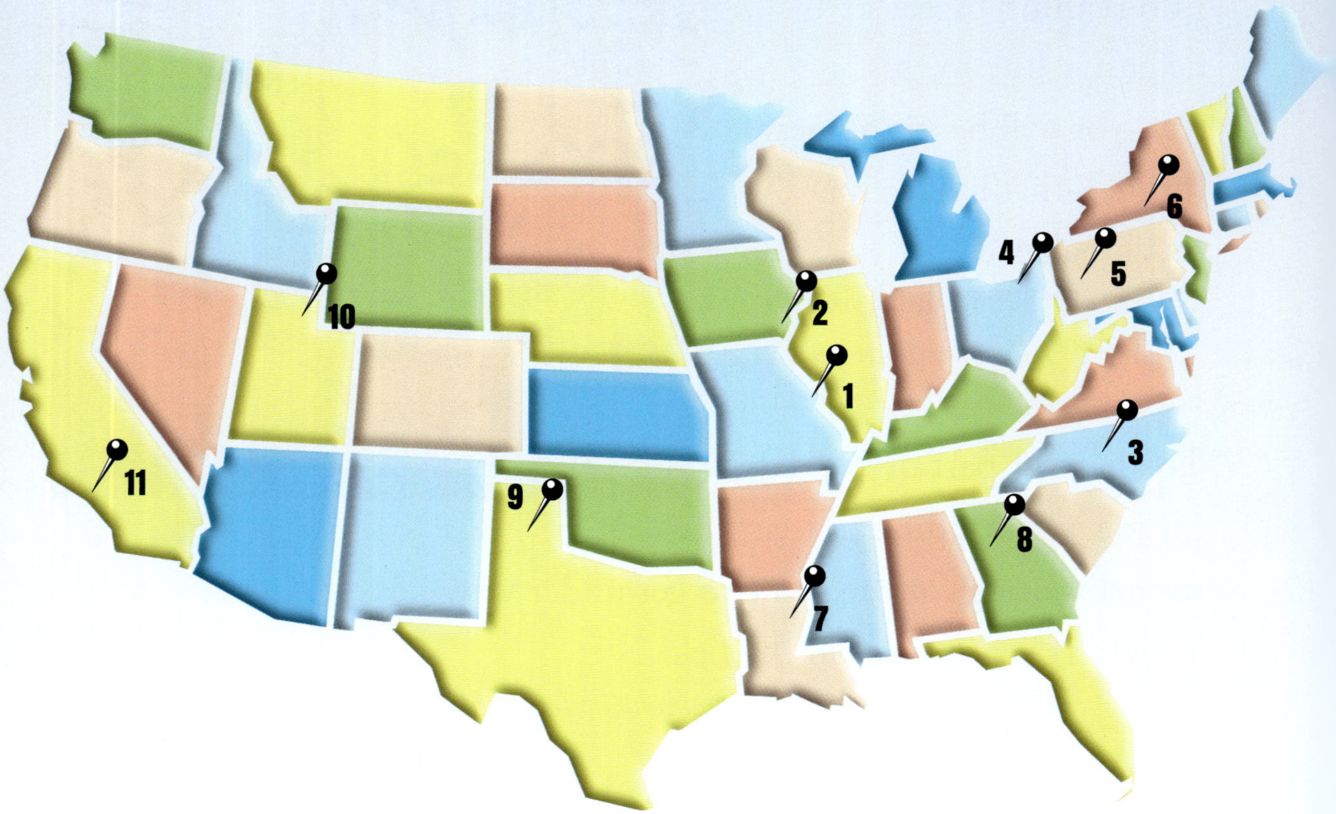

TEAM FACTS

1. **ST. LOUIS, MISSOURI**—The team played here from 1995 to 2014.
2. **BURLINGTON, IOWA**—Kurt Warner was born here.
3. **GREENSBORO, NORTH CAROLINA**—Torry Holt was born here.
4. **CLEVELAND, OHIO**—The team played here from 1937 to 1945.
5. **PITTSBURGH, PENNSYLVANIA**—Aaron Donald was born here.
6. **ELMIRA, NEW YORK**—Bob Waterfield was born here.
7. **MONROE, LOUISIANA**—James Harris was born here.
8. **ATLANTA, GEORGIA**—The Rams won Super Bowl XXXIV here.
9. **PLAINVIEW, TEXAS**—Lawrence McCutcheon was born here.
10. **LOGAN, UTAH**—Merlin Olsen was born here.
11. **LOS ANGELES, CALIFORNIA**—The team played here from 1946 to 1994, and returned to Southern California in 2016.
12. **GUADALAJARA, MEXICO**—Tom Fears was born here.
13. **LAGOS, NIGERIA**—Samson Ekubam was born here.

James Harris

HONOR ROLL

The great Rams teams and players have left their marks on the record books. These are the best of the best!

RAMS ACHIEVEMENTS

ACHIEVEMENT	YEAR
NFL West Champions	1945
NFL Champions	1945
NFL West Champions	1949
NFL West Champions	1950
NFL West Champions	1951
NFL Champions	1951
NFL West Champions	1955
NFC Champions	1979
NFC Champions	1999
Super Bowl XXXIV Champions	1999
NFC Champions	2001
NFC Champions	2018
NFC Champions	2021
Super Bowl LVI Champions	2021

ABOVE: Fans bought this program at the 1951 championship game.

RIGHT: Only a handful of pennants from the team's days in Cleveland have survived.

RAMS AWARD WINNERS

WINNER	AWARD	SEASON
Parker Hall	NFL MVP	1939
Bob Waterfield	NFL MVP	1945
Dan Towler	Pro Bowl MVP	1952
Roman Gabriel	NFL MVP	1969
Roman Gabriel	Pro Bowl Offensive MVP	1969
Merlin Olsen	Pro Bowl Defensive MVP	1969
James Harris	Pro Bowl MVP	1975
Eric Dickerson	Offensive Rookie of the Year	1983
Eric Dickerson	Offensive Player of the Year	1986
Jerry Gray	Pro Bowl MVP	1990
Jerome Bettis	Offensive Rookie of the Year	1993
Marshall Faulk	Offensive Player of the Year	1999
Kurt Warner	NFL MVP	1999
Kurt Warner	Super Bowl MVP	1999
Marshall Faulk	Offensive Player of the Year	2000
Marshall Faulk	NFL MVP	2000
Marshall Faulk	Offensive Player of the Year	2001
Kurt Warner	NFL MVP	2001
Marc Bulger	Pro Bowl Offensive MVP	2004
Sam Bradford	Offensive Rookie of the Year	2010
Todd Gurley	Offensive Rookie of the Year	2015
Aaron Donald	Defensive Player of the Year	2017
Todd Gurley	Offensive Player of the Year	2017
Aaron Donald	Defensive Player of the Year	2018
Aaron Donald	Defensive Player of the Year	2020
Cooper Kupp	Offensive Player of the Year	2021
Cooper Kupp	Super Bowl MVP	2021
Jared Verse	Defensive Rookie of the Year	2024

Kurt Warner warms up before a game.

Quarterback Sam Bradford was the team's third Offensive Rookie of the Year.

PAYDIRT!

Whenever the Rams have the football, their fans root for them to "hit paydirt." The saying dates back more than 100 years to the old prospecting days. It is the layer of earth that contains the first bits of gold. In the NFL, touchdowns are the name of the game. Paydirt is the reward for digging deep and doing the hard work it takes to cross the goal line.

For several years beginning in the 1940s, the Rams often used more than one quarterback in a game. For example, in 1950 the team split their passing duties between Bob Waterfield and Norm Van Brocklin. That season, Van Brocklin threw 18 touchdown passes and Waterfield threw 11. The total of 29 would have been a team record if only one player had thrown all of those passes—and it would have lasted until 1980, when Vince Ferragamo threw 30. Only four other Rams have thrown for more than 30: Jim Everett, Jared Goff, Kurt Warner, and Matthew Stafford.

Warner and Stafford share the team record, with 41. Warner threw 41 TD passes in 1999, when he also set new team marks for completions and passing yards. It was his first year in the NFL

as a starting quarterback. Warner had some of the best targets in the NFL, including Isaac Bruce, Torry Holt, and Marshall Faulk. Stafford threw 41 scoring passes in 2021, in his first year with the Rams. He led them to the Super Bowl championship that season.

Stafford's favorite target was Cooper Kupp. Kupp led the league with 145 catches and 16 touchdowns. While the 145 catches in 2021 set a new team record, the 16 touchdowns did not. That record still belongs to Elroy "Crazy Legs" Hirsch, who scored 17 in 1951. Hirsch led the league in receptions, yards, and yards per catch at a time when the schedule was just 12 games long.

The Rams' record for rushing touchdowns is 18 and it was set in 1983 by Eric Dickerson. Dickerson was in his first year as a pro, but he was no ordinary rookie. He led the NFL with 1,808 rushing yards that season and added two receiving touchdowns for a total of 20. Marshall Faulk equaled Dickerson' team record in 2000. Faulk also had eight touchdown catches for a total of 26. No other Ram has come close to that mark.

ABOVE: Isaac Bruce celebrates a Super Bowl touchdown by Torry Holt.

GLOSSARY

FOOTBALL WORDS
VOCABULARY WORDS

FOOTBALL WORDS

- ALL-PRO—An honor given to the best players at each position. A "first-team" All-Pro is the best of the best.
- ARENA FOOTBALL LEAGUE—A professional league that operated from 1987 to 2019. It used a smaller field and only eight players a side.
- DIVISION—A group of teams that make up a football conference.
- END ZONE—The area behind the goal line. The end zone is 10 yards deep.
- END-AROUND—A trick play where the quarterback hands off to a receiver.
- NATIONAL FOOTBALL CONFERENCE (NFC)—One of two groups of teams that make up the NFL.
- NATIONAL FOOTBALL LEAGUE (NFL)—The league that began in 1920 and is still playing today.
- PLAYOFFS—The series of games after the regular season that lead to the championship game.
- PRESEASON—The period before teams play their first official game. Preseason games do not count in the standings.
- PRO BOWL—The NFL's all-star game.
- ROOKIE—A player in his first professional season.
- SUPER BOWL—The annual championship game of pro football. The first Super Bowl was played following the 1966 season.
- T-FORMATION—An offensive set that positions multiple running backs behind the quarterback, forming a "T."
- TOUCHBACK—A kick that is downed in the end zone by the receiving team.

VOCABULARY WORDS

- *ACADEMY AWARD*—An honor given to someone who worked on a movie as an actor, or in any number of jobs behind the camera.
- *ATTRIBUTE*—An important characteristic or quality.
- *DECADE*—A period of ten years.
- *EXCEPTION*—Something that is unusual or doesn't follow a rule.
- *INFLUENCERS*—People with large social media followings.
- *INNOVATIVE*—Full of new ideas.
- *LOGO*—A design or symbol used by a business.
- *OUTDATED*—No longer current or modern.
- *PIONEERS*—People who are among the first to try a new idea.
- *SAFETY*—A play that awards two points to the defense.

ABOUT THE AUTHOR

MARK STEWART has written more than 75 books for kids on pro and college football. He grew up in New York City rooting for the Giants and Jets, and was lucky enough to meet players from both teams. Mark comes from a publishing family. His parents edited and wrote for national magazines and his grandfather was Sunday Editor of *The New York Times*. After graduating with a degree in history from Duke University, Mark wrote for sports and lifestyle magazines and published his first book in 1992. Since then, he has profiled more than 1,000 athletes, many of whom were Rams—including Flipper Anderson, Kenny Britt, Marc Bulger, Jim Collins, Marshall Faulk, Roman Gabriel, Rosey Grier, Crazy Legs Hirsch, Leroy Irvin, Ray Malavasi, Merlin Olsen, Ricky Proehl, Herb Rich, and Jackie Slater. Mark also wrote *Can't Keep Him Down*, a biography of quarterback Kurt Warner.

ON THE ROAD

THE LOS ANGELES RAMS

1001 Stadium Dr.
Inglewood, CA 90301

THE PRO FOOTBALL HALL OF FAME

2121 George Halas Dr.
NW Canton, Ohio 44708
www.profootballhof.com

ON THE BOOKSHELF

To learn more about the sport of football, look for these books at your library or bookstore:

- Berglund, Bruce. *Football GOATs: The Greatest Athletes of All Time.* North Mankato, MN: Capstone Publishing/Sports Illustrated for Kids, 2022.
- Von Kuczkowski, Alex. *Football: The Ultimate Book.* Dusseldorf, Germany: teNeues Verlag GmbH, 2025.
- Zweig, Eric. *It's A Numbers Game: Football.* Washington, DC: National Geographic Kids, 2022.

INDEX

PAGE NUMBERS IN **BOLD** REFER TO ILLUSTRATIONS.